The
Hot
Sauce
Madness
Love
Burn
Suite

# The
## Hot
### Sauce
#### Madness
### Love
#### Burn
##### Suite

**814 couplets about hot sauce**

## Stephen Cramer

SERVING
HOUSE
BOOKS

The Hot Sauce Madness Love Burn Suite

Copyright © 2020 by Stephen Cramer

All Rights Reserved

Published by Serving House Books
Copenhagen, Denmark and South Orange, NJ
www.servinghousebooks.com

ISBN: 978-1-947175-36-5

Library of Congress Control Number: 2020947358

No part of this book may be used or reproduced in any manner whatsoever without the prior written permission of the copyright holder except for brief quotations in critical articles or reviews.

Member of The Independent Book Publishers Association

First Serving House Books Edition 2020

Cover Design: Michael Balzano

Author Photograph: Holly Brevent

Serving House Books Logo: Barry Lereng Wilmont

For the first person to take a second bite.

# Also by Stephen Cramer

*Shiva's Drum*
*Tongue & Groove*
*From the Hip*
*A Little Thyme & a Pinch of Rhyme*
*Bone Music*
*A Jar of Moon Air: Selected Poems of Jaime Sabines,*
    (tr. with Alejandro Merizalde)
*Turn It Up! Music in Poetry from Jazz to Hip-Hop*
    (editor)

# Contents

## I.

| | |
|---|---|
| Chili | 11 |
| Mistakes | 12 |
| You'll Always Remember Your First | 14 |
| The Scoville Scale | 16 |
| Pain | 19 |
| Wings | 21 |
| Hottest | 23 |
| Spelling | 25 |
| Sambal Oelek | 27 |
| Homemade | 29 |
| Avery Island | 31 |
| Addiction | 34 |
| Shapes | 36 |
| George Washington's Missed Opportunity | 38 |
| Sriracha | 40 |
| Capsicum | 42 |

## II.

| | |
|---|---|
| Shishito | 47 |
| Pimiento | 48 |
| Banana Pepper | 49 |
| Paprika | 50 |
| Poblano | 51 |
| Anaheim | 53 |
| Mirasol | 55 |
| Chery Bomb | 57 |
| Jalapeño | 58 |
| Serrano | 60 |
| Chile de Arbol | 62 |

Cayenne             64
Aji Limo            66
Tabasco             68
Piquín              70
Bird's Eye Chili    71
Chiltepin           73
Datil               75
Habanero            77
Scotch Bonnet       80
Red Savina          82
Bhut Jolokia        84
Trinidad Scorpion   86
Carolina Reaper     88
Pepper X            90

III.

Fruit               95
Origins             97
Pico de Gallo       99
Heat Scale          101
Extract             102
Mole                104
Chipotle            106
Capsaicin           107
Cajuns              108
Xnipec              110
Wind Chilies        112
Vitamin C           113
Ristras             114
The Big Five        115
Harissa             117
Weaning             118
Antidote            119

Bibliography        121
About the Author    123

I

# Chili

The word hails
from Nahuatl,

the Aztec language that
gave us *chocolate,*

*peyote, avocado,*
*tomato.*

During
spiritual fasting,

the Aztecs
abstained from sex

& chilies, & only conjecture
can tell us which was harder

to renounce. Chili:
the least chilly

bite
ever to light

up the back of your throat,
lips, rim of tongue, to the most

glorious tinder. Blink,
& you see sequins,

& then the spicy
love scene turns into a heist.

## Mistakes

Columbus mistook, we
all know, the natives he

found when he landed for
"Indians," though where

he landed in Venezuela
is 9,439 miles from India.

Then he called
the spice the natives used

*pimiento* (black pepper)
though it's never

been even closely
related to the peppercorn that he

had hoped to find (*piper
nigrum*, black pepper,

the so-called
*black gold*,

the most prized
spice

of the day). What he
found instead was capsicum. We

all make
mistakes,

dousing food with
sauce before first tasting it,

only to find
that it turned

the plate of piled nachos
almost

inevitably
inedibly

molten. Proverb: *don't test
the river's depth*

*with both feet.* Be cautious, it means,

but do we
listen? No. Like early

explorers, we survive
by jumping to conclusions. We dive.

## You'll Always Remember Your First

Early days as a grad
school "chef," that Harlem pad

on Convent
Ave., with the slant

to the floors & only
my own palate to please,

my food's palette veered
toward the hotter

colors: apricot, lemon,
flame, crimson,

the pile of peppers
spilled out on the counter.

The late 90s saw
my first hot sauce

obsession: the Goya liberal
on my two-course meal:

the rice wok-fried,
half seasoned

with soy sauce,
the other half doused

with hot sauce. I grew,
those years, into

an explorer of that culinary
*terra incognita*, the Death Valley

of the throat, my
mouth caught between two high

noons. This was the daily
rendezvous, the nightly

gamble & sting
of the tongue.

## The Scoville Scale

1912: pharmacist Wilbur
Lincoln Scoville first

measured
the "heat" of peppers

(the word's in quotes
because there's no

actual heat in this
equation, just spiciness,

which hoodwinks
our bodies into thinking

physical flames are
licking our

tongues, throat, lips).
Chilies aren't *caliente*, which

implies
heat from an actual fire,

but *picante*,
the word we

use for heat that arises
from spice.

Scoville units are calculated
based on how diluted

a pepper has to be
before the heat

no longer registers
on the tongue. Another

way to test the heat is
with the tip of your penis,

as I did unwittingly
one day, when I

was chopping peppers
for a sauce in our

old Queens apartment. I chopped
& chopped, then made a quick pitstop

in the bathroom, where
my fingers transferred

the burn to a place
with... let's just say

many many times as many
nerve cells, which prompted me

to run to the fridge, to
open a new

container
of sour

cream, & stick it
in. In lieu of this

method I'm all for maintaining
Scoville's scale. Save

the rest of the body
for all the extraordinary

things the rest of the body can
do. I washed my hands

while that sting of stings
abated, then I went back to chopping.

# Pain

Leopold von Sacher-
Masoch, the writer

bewitched by our love of pain,
& whose name

spurred
our word

*masochism*, understood not only
how pain says to our body

*stop* (trying to keep
us alive) but also how we

so blissfully
disobey.

Most of us mess with pain
in the most secure ways:

roller coaster, bungee
jump, horror movie,

because suffering so often links arms
with pleasure. The sweat's welcome:

brow, upper
lip, the weather

of all your hidden
creases gone

muggy.
Your body,

imagining physical heat,
tries to cool off, inducing sweat,

tears, the mucous
slick beneath your nose,

but the palpitations are
pleasing, the tears

a hot & saline
thrill. The rope burn

pierces
your throat with a blaze so fierce

that your middle name
turns to Napalm.

# Wings

Drop a spring seed not
into loam & rich dirt

but into a raging fire—
that's a fair

analogy for how our bodies
treat the pepper seeds

we devour.
Our

digestive systems
dismantle roots, stems,

seeds with their acids, & render
the fruit fruitless. No wonder

the peppers
have evolved to burn

us: our bodies
refuse to help them carry

on. But capsaicin doesn't disturb
the digestive tracts of birds

because they actually
*do* help, distributing the seeds,

unharmed, across field, pasture
& meadow. Nothing's better

(for the peppers or
for us) than having the peppers

flown to a patch of soil, then
deposited in a bed

of the bird's ready-made
compost so that they

can go on, so that
the seeds, which lack

any method of flight
or self-propulsion, inherit,

at least for a few exhilarating
moments, wings.

# Hottest

Hard to
say who

is the hottest actor,
athlete, accountant on your

office floor.
Not so with peppers: in 1994

California's
red savina

wore the crown
with a half a million

Scovilles. In 2007
bhut jolokia topped a million.

Trinidad & Tobago's scorpion
in 2012 held on

for a year before
the Carolina reaper

broke 1.5 million.
Selective breeding &

Punnett squares work their mathematical
miracles

for our tongues as we
gradually ratchet up the heat

through the ceiling, through
the roof, then bid *adieu*

to the clouds. We pass the sea
of tranquility &, as our salivary

glands await the next tier,
head on into the stratosphere.

## Spelling

The spelling's as various
as the species in genus

capsicum: *chile* in
Central &

South America (so
as not to

be confused with
chili, the dish

served *con* or *sin*
*carne*), *chilli* in

England & India,
& *chili* (or *chile*) in the

States. Some argue the original
transliteration from the Nahuatl

(by Dr. Francisco Hernandez, 1514-
1578) was *chilli,*

in which case, the word was
probably once

pronounced *chee-yee*. But ask
someone to pass

you the chee-yee
sauce & they'll give you a funny

look, & so we embrace
yet another mistake

& ask for the *chill-E*
sauce so that we

can experience the
taste bud supernova.

## Sambal Oelek

A *sambal*'s an
Indonesian

chili-based
sauce or paste,

& *oelek* (sounding
tantalizingly

close to
*you*

*lick*) refers
to the mortar

& pestle used to
grind the peppers into

vinegar & salt,
the pestle held with a light

hand so as not to fully
crush the seeds

during that circular wrist
motion, so you get

to crunch the seeds
between

your molars like they're
the most fiery caviar,

the sauce more than
brackish, briney as an

olive, something that
makes you want

to say *oelek, oelek, oelek*
as you lick & lick. You lick.

## Homemade

My recipe's simple: vinegar,
garlic, peppers, salt, & sugar,

all boiled
then blended

up & poured
into beer bottles (clear

in order to show
off that sunset color). (No

tomato, you ask? No carrots? No
blueberries or mangos?

Hey, I love a salad.
I just don't need

to have a salad in my hot sauce.)
The least inconvenience

in the history of
inconveniences: you have

to drain beer
bottles in order

to have receptacles for
the sauce, so the hotter

the kitchen gets,
the more beer you must

consume. Cap 'em,
let 'em cool, & then

they can take their
place among all the other

bottles stored
on the fridge door

like a mini-Manhattan, their heights
rouged as if by twilight.

## Avery Island

Anhinga, ibis, bufflehead,
roseate spoonbill, hooded

merganser,
coot, shoveler:

cinnamon teal,
northern pintail—

none of them
consume

the hundreds of acres
of capsaicin-filled pods. Warblers,

wood stork, black crowned night
heron, swallow-tailed kite,

gallinule, stilt, avocet... 1895:
the sanctuary *Bird City* was founded by

Edward Avery
McIlhenny,

son of Tabasco's founder,
to help snowy egrets, endangered

at the time. Late
1800s, snowy egrets

were practically annihilated,
their plumes said

to be the perfect adornment
for women's hats.

So McIlhenny gathered
what egrets he could

on Avery Island. When the birds
headed south to winter

in the Bahamas, Cuba,
& Central America,

he wondered if they went
away for good, if his experiment

was over. The following
spring,

they returned with even more
egrets like an encore

magic trick
where, with a flick

of a wand, one
egret becomes ten.

Now over 100,000
nest on the island.

Those first tabasco
chilies on Avery Island, who

knew if they'd take?
But they took, & day

by day they
return like those egrets, the way

we return to take pull after pull
from those fire-filled bottles.

## Addiction

The sequence is familiar: craving,
indulging,

developing
a tolerance, upping

the dosage &/or
heat. There's always a hotter

pepper,
a greater

fix when
the most recent

no longer
cuts it for

you. But they
induce no chemical dependency,

& the benefits are legion: hot
peppers fight

inflammation & obesity,
increase metabolism, & have three

times as much
vitamin C as oranges. You just

might have to consider
when you eat hot peppers

that you're
increasing your

lifespan not
shortening it.

Enjoy more,
& live longer.

You don't get
to eat

more sauce when
you're dead.

## Shapes

Banana, dimpled
heart, dreidel,

mini pumpkin,
russet tear, crimson

icicle, diminutive tomato,
waxen rose, torpedo,

contorted prune,
scimitar, wrinkled crown,

blimp, emerald acorn,
rocket, goat horn,

static flame, squat jelly
bean, tapered cone. I'm

no shapist & so
will eat you no

matter
whether

you're
slender

& sweaty, or a barb
& sickle, a crinkled bulb

with a scorpion tail
that feels

like it's both
100 proof

& a four
alarm fire.

## George Washington's Missed Opportunity

Though in 1785 George Washington
grew cayenne peppers in

his Mount Vernon,
Virginia garden,

the pepper
never

made
its way

into the recipes
in Martha Washington's *Book of Cookery*.

Let's consider that
disappointment

number
one. & sure,

he was a delegate
to the first

Continental Congress, led the Continental Army
in the Revolutionary

War, had strong showings in
Valley Forge & Yorktown,

& created
the United

States Navy, but in another
disappointment, four

years after
he grew those peppers,

when
he became the first president,

he could have but didn't vote
to make them the national fruit.

## Sriracha

Almost as much as your
flavor,

I love how your
ingredients are

listed in no less than
five different languages on

the back of your bottle.
You need no commercials

to spread the word for
you, because your

taste does
the talking. I love

how your
most popular

U.S. brand
(Huy Fong) is named

after the ship your
founder

took from
Vietnam

to the United States.
I love how, before he came

to the U.S., he made
the sauce in Gerber baby

food jars. But I hate to
think of any child whose

parent might have fed
them this by accident.

It's a long way from mashed
peaches & squash.

# Capsicum

Joseph Pitton de
Tournefourt, the 17th century

French botanist,
provided the genus

with its name. A founder,
as it were,

of systematic
botany, he discovered the trick

of defining the difference
between genus

& species: binomialism
born. Some say the word's from

the Latin *capsa*, meaning
*box*, (possibly referencing

the hollowness of peppers)
while others say it's more

likely from the Greek *kapto*,
meaning *to bite*. I vote for *to*

*bite*, but even at that
some argue that it's about

you biting the pepper,
whereas I'm much more

captivated by
the way the pepper bites

you back. Degrees:
your tongue feels

like it's 1,000 while your
stomach gives you the third.

II

# Shishito

*50-200 Scoville units*

They say the shishito
looks like a lion's head, so

the word's a cross between
the Japanese

*shishi* (lion) & *togarashi*
(chili pepper), but to me

the name's onomatopoeic for
the sizzling of the peppers

as they're sautéed with olive oil
& salt, or broiled

to blister & char the skin
with heat. In this

game of culinary
roulette, 19 of 20'll be

mild, though that one
outlier'll make your tongue

& throat sizzle like the peppers
being sautéed, will turn

your mouth into the sizzling glow
of the word *shishito*.

# Pimiento

*100-500 Scoville units*

The name *pimiento*
(also *pimento*)

refers to this pepper's
bright color

(see the English
word *pigment*). Stuffed into a Spanish

or Greek green olive, these
transform into the traditional martini

garnish, one of them speared by
a toothpick (two if you've been kind

to your bartender).
tip: always be kind to your

bartender,
& not just to earn

this double splash
of color, this lack

of heat that's shown
up, outdone,

all but subsumed by
the vodka's fire.

## Banana Pepper

*100-500 Scoville units*

Also known as
the yellow wax

pepper, these are commonly pickled,
& often found

on pizza, where they're
really just a vehicle for vinegar.

Who hasn't made
rings of these peppers? If you raised

your hand, it's probably
time to marry

the heat & start decking
yourself out with piquant bling.

# Paprika

*250-1,000 Scoville units*

Often dried & ground into powder
(sweet, spicy, or smoked) this pepper

(or these peppers, since no
single variety is used to

make this
spice)

first hit Hungary in
the 1600s. Paprika's now the Hungarian

national spice. Kalocsa
& Szeged, the

two Hungarian
cities, have been

competing for centuries for the title
of Paprika Capital

of the World. Some of these peppers
are the burn of a match, others

keep the match
safely in its sheath,

& still others are the extravagance
of the whole matchbook going up at once.

# Poblano

*1,000-2,000 Scoville units*

Named
after the state

they hail from (Puebla, Mexico),
this pepper's often dried, & then known

as an ancho, which means *wide*
(they're flattened when dried

& thus broader).
Looking like dark

green bell peppers
on a diet, these are

best known in the form of *chiles
rellenos* (stuffed chilies),

in which they're roasted,
charred, skinned,

stuffed with cheese, battered
& fried, then drenched

in tomato sauce. I'd
say it's like

an Italian pizza in a smoky pocket
of spice, but

tomatoes
also

originated in a
field in South America.

# Anaheim

*500-2,500 Scoville units*

1896: after a visit to New Mexico,
Emilio

Ortega (not only
former sheriff of Ventura County,

but also of the household
Mexican brand)

brought a few seeds home
& planted them near Anaheim,

& lo & behold
they flourished in the gold

rush of California sun.
The pepper's called

*Anaheim* after where Ortega
first grew them. Now, the

city's since been
buried under Disneyland.

Eating this pepper can
feel like ascending Space Mountain,

an absolute roller
coaster

for
your

palate, & hey,
you never had to wait

in
line.

# Mirasol

*2,500-5,000 Scoville Units*

*Looking at the sun*
the name means,

because mirasol
peppers grow

upright,
downright

begging birds
to disperse their seeds.

(Dried, they're known
as *guajillo*,

or
*little gourd*

because the seeds
rattle in the dried

pod. They
are second only

to anchos for dried pepper
usage in Mexico.) Mirasols are

one of the most popular
peppers

for *mole
sauce*. Incidentally,

saying mole
sauce is as redundant as saying

*bright sun*, the kind
of bright sun you'd find

mirasol peppers in as they
reach for the sky all day.

## Cherry Bomb

> *3,000-5,000 Scoville units*

It looks more like a squat
tomato than a cherry &, though hot,

the name packs far more
heat than the actual pepper,

which is why it's good
for stuffing with goat

cheese & breadcrumbs
& garlic & mushrooms

& whatever else you can fit
in their little

container, their little bin
of little capsaicin.

## Jalapeño

*2,500-8,000 Scoville units*

The Nahuatl word *Xalapa*—
from the roots *xālli* (sand) & *āpan*

(water place)—
is the source

of the name
of Veracruz's capitol, which became

the source
of this pepper.

Some call it
*chili gordo* (the fat

chili), & it's often
picked green,

before it's fully
ripe. Corking: those grey

lightning-like lines
you might find

on a jalapeño, those thin
streaks formed because the skin

can't keep up with
the pepper's growth.

Some call them *scarring*
or *stretch-marks*, & many in

the U.S. see them as
flaws,

but south of the border
they're considered

tokens of excellence—the more
corking

the more
heat. They like their peppers

the way I like my
people: scarred but still fiery.

## Serrano

*10,000-23,000 Scoville units*

*Mountainous*, the word
means in Spanish, as the pepper

was birthed in no
valley but in the sierras of Mexico.

Smaller
& skinnier

than a jalapeño, it's
got a greater kick.

So on a Scoville chart the jalapeño
might be a valley, while a serrano

would be a mountain, maybe not
Everest, but a high sierra

ready to deliver the flavor
of its rarified air

to your mouth,
& you look down

on those valleys
panting, each

breath burning more than the last,
& what some have

called *gustatory perspiration*
dappling

(or one could
say *peppering*) your forehead.

## Chile De Arbol

> *15,000-30,000 Scoville units*

Also known as the bird's beak (*pico
de pajaro*)

& the rat's
tail chili (*cola de rata*),

neither of which sound very
appetizing to me,

its name comes from the Spanish
*tree chili* (though it's

a bush) because of its
thick

& woody stem.
The pepper looks like a slim

& miniature
cayenne, but it's smokier

& has less bite. Though they're often
found in

ristras (strings of dried
chilies or garlic, preserved

for later use)
or interwoven into

wreathes, I prefer
their flavor

weaving around
my tongue &

throat in loops & braids
& burning figure eights.

# Cayenne

*30,000-50,000 Scoville Units*

Some say
this pepper was named

by Columbus
who labeled it as

such after the city Cayenne
in French Guiana.

Other say
the city

was named after the peppers.
Still others

theorize
that it arises

from the word *quiinia*
(from the Brazilian

Tupi language for
*pepper*)

(which makes
the phrase

*cayenne pepper* unfortunately
perfectly

redundant).
With the perfect

mix of heat & flavor,
the ideal fit for

southern
weather,

it's hard not to call cayenne a
king of peppers in Louisiana.

## Aji Limo

*30,000-50,000 Scoville units*

From the Peruvian
Andes, this pepper's name means

*Lima Pepper*,
after

the capital city of Peru,
though you'd

be forgiven for
thinking it referred

to its notes of citrus when
cooked, or even

its yellow
appearance. After all, it's also

known as Lemon Drop, a name
which persists from the earliest days

when the pepper
first

arrived
in the United

States, & it was erroneously
labeled *aji*

*limón*
(lemon

pepper). Some say it doesn't matter,
that the sense of taste is superior

to the written word,
because flavor

has no need for
translation. & it's true I'd rather

eat a pepper
than the word

*pepper* every
time.

# Tabasco

*30,000-50,000 Scoville units*

Cultivated in Tabasco,
Mexico,

& transplanted to Louisiana
in the 1840s, this pepper's the

base of the eponymous
sauce.

In the late 1850s, Colonel
Maunsell

White gifted Edmund
McIlhenny some

tabasco peppers. McIlhenny
planted them on Avery

Island, Louisiana, but the Civil War
quickly terminated any future

he might have imagined with
them. He & his

family moved to Texas.
1865: the war ended,

& he returned
to find his plantation ravaged,

the crops smashed. Miraculously,
a few chilies

made it through. He
planted more from the seeds.

1868: Edmund
McIlhenny found

that cologne bottles
were the desirable vessels

for his sauce, their necks thin so
as to dole

out only a single drop at a time,
their insides

cleaned so any trace
of their previous

inhabitants
were ghosts. He sent

out the bottles to store
owners, who immediately bought more

to sell, & the craze
was on. In 1946, the name

*Tabasco* became the sole property
of the McIlhenny Company.

McIlhenny was the creator,
but the vinegar's

the salesman
& the heat's the delivery man.

# Piquín

*30,000-60,000 Scoville units*

Also: *pequín*,
(pronounced *puh-KEEN*)

the name of these
nubs of heat

comes from the Spanish *pequeño*,
meaning: *small*. Smoke

a pile of lemons
& oranges, &

add some bite,
& you'll approximate

the flavor
of this pepper.

Smoked in Nicaragua, the piquín
is known

as *diente
de*

*perro* (dog's teeth), not
just because of their shape but

also because the hotter
peppers

have a bit more
bite than bark.

# Bird's Eye Chili

*50,000-100,000 Scoville units*

Also called *Thai chilis*, these peppers,
sometimes as small as your

fingernail & similar to the African
peri-peri, are mostly found

in Southeast Asia & are
popular

in Thai & Vietnamese
dishes.

Some say
their name

comes from their
size (which is barely larger

than the eye of a bird),
others

from the fact that birds
disseminate them, which makes more

sense to me, though it has less
to do with their eyes

than their tongues,
which remain unstung

by capsaicin,
allowing the seeds in turn

to experience transportation
in

a winged
vegetal migration.

# Chiltepin

*50,000- 100,000 Scoville Units*

This pepper's name
(also *chile tepin*) derives from

the Nahuatl
words *chile* & *tecpintl*,

or *flea
chili*

because of its
diminutive size.

Tiny & round, this is
the only wild chili indigenous

to the U.S.,
growing from Arizona to Texas.

Many consider
this pepper

to be the ancestor
of the first

cultivated chilies. Just a quarter
inch in diameter,

their heat hits
hard & fast, but it

mellows
quickly. Try to grow

them commercially & you'll
fail,

so finding
a wild bush of them in

the southwest is an unequalled
treasure, like striking gold.

# Datil

*100,000-300,000 Scoville units*

From St. Augustine,
Florida, America's oldest continually

inhabited city, this
pepper looks like a habanero with a thin

waistline, a habanero
on a diet. Also known

as the *yellow lantern*,
it's as hot as a hab, but with a sweeter,

fruity kick. 1513:
St. Augustine

was founded by
Ponce de Leon, who was trying

to find the legendary
fountain of youth. Many

studies show that those who
enjoy spicy foods

live longer, because chilies
are antioxidant, fight obesity,

promote digestion &
reduce the chances

of heart disease.
So maybe

Ponce de Leon
really did find the fountain

of youth, &
its name is *capsaicin*.

# Habanero

*100,000-350,000 Scoville units*

Sometimes this
pepper is

spelled, mistakenly,
*habañero*, the tilde added by

those who
see the word *jalapeño*

& are searching for
consistency in their lives. Born

in
the Amazon,

the hab was dispersed by Spanish
colonists

so far & wide that
18th century Dutch

botanist Nikolaus Joseph von Jacquin
thought it originated in

China. Thus his species name for
the pepper,

*chinense* (Chinese), a moniker
which has stuck over

the years,
even since we knew better.

Its common name comes
from

the capital city of Cuba,
Habana,

known in the U.S. as
Havana, because

many
believe

it traveled
west to Central

& South America
from Cuba.

1999:
it reigned

as the world's hottest pepper,
before

the fiery flood of bhut jolokia,
Trinidad scorpion, & Carolina

reaper. Still,
you might not be able

to phone in a smile or even
a breath when

you take a swig
or a slug

of this pepper
sauce then

send out a useless
S.O.S.

## Scotch Bonnet

*80,000-400,000 Scoville units*

Named for its
resemblance to the Scottish

tam o'shanter
hat, this pepper's

crinkled
& flattened

as though it had
been trampled.

It sounds like a grandmother
of a hot pepper—

dainty, even
fragile—but not so when

you take a bite. A variety
of habanero, it's more commonly

found in Caribbean food than
Central & South American.

One bite
tells your mind to take a hike,

makes your
shoulders

spread
with chills like you just sprouted

wings. It begins
that ticker tape parade of endorphins,

& shoots flaming
asterisks into your brain.

## Red Savina

*350,000-577,000 Scoville units*

Another variety
of hab, this one was bred by

Frank Garcia
Jr. in Walnut, California.

1989, the story goes that a bunch
of cheap buyers made a pitch

to pay
half price for 30

acres of habaneros,
so

the farmer
decided to plow it under.

He stepped onto his tractor,
but just before

he revved the engine he spotted
a single red

pepper among the hundreds
& hundreds of orange ones. He planted

the mutant's seeds & soon
amassed acres of this new

red pepper:
red savina. From 1994-

2006, it was the world's hottest
pepper, & you can bet

that buyers were about
to pay a lot

more than half price
for it, to be jinxed by that light-

ning in a bottle
& have their whole

mouths go tropical, to have the burn
pick up velocity—smolder

& gasp—& the pepper
shove their

funny bone
sideways down their throats.

## Bhut Jolokia

*850,000-1,000,000 Scoville units*

Two times hotter
than the previous hottest pepper

(the red savina), bhut jolokia
didn't so much knock

on its door but
blow the door right

off its hinges &
incinerate it in

a conflagration of capsaicin.
It's also known

as naga jolokia (in
Sanskrit *naga* means *serpent*

or *cobra*,
& *jolokia*

means *flame* or *burn*)
& the ghost pepper. *Bhut* means

*ghost* in Assamese (an
Indo-Aryan language in

India), maybe
applicable because the heat

can ambush you, take you by
surprise

like a ghost. From 2007-
2010,

it was, according to Guinness,
the world's hottest

pepper. It's been
said that Indians rub it on

their fences to keep elephants at
bay, which makes me think that

an awful lot
of us would come up short

in an IQ test against
an elephant

because here
we are

willingly pouring
it onto our

rice &
beans.

## Trinidad Scorpion

*1,200,000- 2,000,000 Scoville units*

March 3rd, 2011
till August 7,

2013:
the Trinidad Scorpion

"Butch T" was the hottest
pepper known on earth.

Named by Neil Smith (of The Hippy
Seed Company)

after his seed supplier
(Butch Taylor

of Mississippi's
Zydeco Farms), those seeds

(originally
from T&T)

sport, on
their bottoms, a scorpion's

tail. Eat one, & regret's
an impossible antidote,

but this is the Hades
you always

wanted to take
a tour of. Your brain

may calculate
every possible escape

route that doesn't exist,
but in the end you're fenced in

by the stench
of Cerberus' breath.

## Carolina Reaper

*1,400,000-2,200,000 Scoville units*

Frankensteiningly cross a bhut
jolokia with a crazy hot

habanero, & you get the pepper
named after

the scythe-
wielding skeleton who severs our lives

with a single
sickled

swing.
The creation of Smokin'

Ed Currie
of Puckerbutt Pepper Company,

this gnarled angel
of death is here to tell

you your time
has come.

2003: the reaper swiped
the headlines

from the Trinidad scorpion,
its single barb on

the bottom ready not
just to take your soul but

to pierce your stomach lining,
the initial burn a dim foreshadowing

of a flagrant
*dénouement,*

in which no parts
of your mouth or soul are

safe. Take a bite, everything
becomes flame, & you enter a burning

room with a jukebox that's filled with discs
of fire instead of music.

## Pepper X

*3,100,000 Scoville units*

Here's another creation
of Smokin'

Ed Currie, the same
amazing,

lovely, &
masochistic guy who created

the
Carolina

Reaper.
The pepper's

found in The Last
Dab,

the culmination
of Hot Ones

from Season 4 to
the present (2020). Easy enough to blow

a sauce's Scovilles through
the roof

with an addition
of oleoresin

extract,
but

this sauce comes by
the extreme heat naturally.

So let yourself be dared
& blackmailed

into taking a bite of this mustard-
colored

miracle,
this practically flammable

fruit, until your
mouth is a structure

fire with no sirens
on their way. This is when

things get surreal, when
you see your own

panicked look multiplied
a thousand

times in
a broken

mirror that you'd
inadvertently swallowed.

III

# Fruit

The word
conjures

the sweetness of guava,
mango, pineapple. But

chilies,
technically,

are also fruit,
the hottest berries known to

the tongue. General
rule: vegetables

usually go seedless, while
fruits like peppers, apples

& pears (& tomato, eggplant,
& zucchini, for that

matter) house them. I'm crazy
for fruit salad, especially

if the fruit's blended up
& mixed with a dressing of

salt, garlic, vinegar,
& maybe a touch of sugar.

The door of my
fridge is populated by

a dozen
spicy fruit salads, each in

their own bottle.
Let us drizzle

these piquant fruit
salads on a litany of foods

that even the Bible would look
upon with envy: mac

& cheese,
& rice & beans,

& pizza, & potatoes,
& tomato

soup, & eggs, & burgers,
& fries, & collard

greens,
& on into infinity.

# Origins

Chili peppers were
cultivated in Latin America as far

back as 5200 B.
C.

That's about 5000 years
before

Greeks built the Parthenon,
over 2000 before some Egyptian

thought it'd be cool
to create giant three dimensional

triangles to honor
their dead pharaohs, 1000 years

before some forward-
thinking individual invented

the wheel. A quick shout
out to that guy. No doubt

the wheel was a game changer,
but sometimes when you're

sitting there
before

a bland meal, it's a tough call
whether the wheel

or chili peppers
have been more

of a boon
for civilization.

## Pico De Gallo

Also called *salsa fresca*
or *salsa cruda*,

*pico de gallo* literally
means *rooster's beak*.

Some say it got its name
because you use your thumb

& forefinger like
beak

to eat it. Others say
that the serranos traditionally

used in his recipe
are curved like a beak.

Because of the colors (the green
chili, the white onion,

& the red tomato)
it's sometimes referred to

as *salsa
bandera*,

or *flag sauce* because it
mimics

the flag of Mexico.
The chunky salsa consists of tomato,

onion, lime juice, cilantro,
& serrano or jalapeño...

Incidentally, Latin Americans
make no distinction

between salsa (uncooked)
& sauce (cooked).

It's all *salsa*, they concur,
south of the border.

# Heat Scale

The Aztecs' heat
scale: *cococ*: hot,

*cocopatic*: very hot (as far as I can
tell, no relation

to the word *copacetic*, though
I know many who

feel most *copacetic*
when ingesting something *cocopatic*).

Then you've got
*cocoquauitl*: extremely hot,

*cocopetztic*: glistening
hot, *cocopetzpatic*: very

glistening hot, & finally
*cocopetzquauitl*: extremely

glistening hot.
Then there's the hot that

goes beyond
words,

from the seven syllables
of *cocopetzquauitl*

to the ultimate & ultimately immense
silence.

## Extract

Oleoresin capsicum (concentrated
oil containing capsaicin) is made

when all pepper
elements that are

not capsaicin
are removed. Cheating?

Maybe. But then again, if
you want to ingest this,

some say it helps to have a
diploma

in Stupid.
It's like ingesting lighter fluid

or
pepper

spray, like falling through some sick
trap door of idiotic

machismo gone wild. Staring
at a spoonful is like watching

yourself about to fall down
a flight of stairs, then

sometime later climbing
back up only to find

the quickest way down
again.

# Mole

The word
*mole*'s adapted

from the Nahuatl, in
which *molli* means

*mixture*. So
*guacamole*: a *mole*

(mixture) of *guaca*
(vegetables). The

myth: once, when the archbishop
was slated to make a stop

at the Santa Clara
convent in Puebla,

the penniless
(or centavoless?)

nuns panicked
with so little food

to offer. They combined
what little they had on hand

& served it on top
of a turkey. The archbishop,

who went wild for these
meager bites, asked for the recipe's

name & was told
it was a *mole*

(a mixture). This velvety lick
of chocolate, cinnamon, garlic,

anise, & cloves, is
spiked by chilies,

the sweetness Trojan-
horsing in the burn.

# Chipotle

A *chipotle*
(the Nahuatl way

to designate *smoked
chili*) is a dried

& smoked jalapeño,
often steeped in adobo

(from the Spanish verb *adobar:
to marinade)*. These peppers

are picked late, when
red, not green,

transferring that
sweet,

late summer
to our

sweetened & stung
tongues.

# Capsaicin

It's not a flavor, capsaicin.
No, it bypasses taste buds &

barrels straight
into your nerves, tipping off your brain

that you're being burned, & the brain
responds by sending throngs of pain-

killing endorphins
& bliss-inducing dopamine

to the rescue. The pain of
eating a pepper does

what meditation's supposed to:
brings the moment into

sharp focus. This fireless burn
is a fire sermon

6,000 years after
the Buddha delivered his: *the eyes are*

*on fire... sounds are on fire...*
*smells are on fire... the body's on fire...*

Let your mouth be a diminutive replica
of the universal pain, & bring on the

heat. As the Buddha says of this world-pyre,
*the tongue is on fire.*

# Cajuns

The outbreak of the French
& Indian War: the British

kicked French Canadian
colonists out of a Nova Scotian

region they called
Acadie. The colonists fled

south to Louisiana, &
referred

to themselves *acadienne*,
which, given

their accent,
transformed into *Cajun*.

One upside
to a forced

migration:
cayenne

peppers, which grew
to be central to

so many cajun
dishes, also loved the southern sun.

It's like the peppers
& people were

equally awaiting the day when
the travelling would end

in the land where cayenne grew,
in this, the tastiest *rendezvous*.

# Xnipec

This Mexican
salsa, made with onions,

habaneros,
tomatoes,

cilantro, & orange juice,
takes its place among a few

rare foods that begin with the letter
x, some others

being xouba (a sardine-ish
fish

from Spanish waters), xigua (an African
melon),

xiaolongbao (a Chinese
steamed bun), & xacuti

(an Indian
curry). Pronounced *Shneepeck*, this Mayan

word translates to *Dog's Nose*,
most likely because,

thanks to those
habaneros,

you'll sweat
like a wet

dog's nose might
as soon as you take a bite.

## Wild Chilies

They tend to point skyward,
offering themselves to birds

who then loan their seeds wings,
dispersing

them across the land.
Domesticated

chilies have no need
for birds, since they've enlisted

humans to
do

the planting for
them. This lets them grow heavier

&, pendulous, hang,
awaiting

the fingers' twist
or the pinch

& gentle
pull.

## Vitamin C

If only Columbus &/or
his fellow sailors

had known
how much vitamin

C those peppers
contained (more

than oranges), they could've chowed
down

on them
& spent so much less time

worrying
about scurvy.

## Ristras

Spanish for "strings,"
ristras are wreathes of drying

peppers
(or

sometimes garlic). Traditionally
their length was based on how much a family

would need to
sustain them through

the winter
& spring (or

until the next growing season).
Convention

dictated that the wreath
should be two times the height

of all your
family members

combined, the hope being that as
you finish that last

pepper, the new year's fresh pods
are turning red in your yard.

## The Big Five

The five major species
of domesticated peppers in genus

capsicum include:
capsicum annuum

(which means
"annual" & makes no sense

because traditionally peppers
are

perennial).
These peppers include bell

pepper, cayenne,
& jalapeño. Then there's c. chinense

(named in
1776 by Nikolaus Joseph von Jaquin,

a Dutch physician who
assumed,

incorrectly,
that these

plants originated in China). This
species

includes habanero, scotch
bonnet,

datil, &
bhut jolokia. Next up is c. frutescens,

which includes tabasco & piri
piri,

then c. baccatum (which means "berry-
like"). These

include Peruvian
aji, Bolivian

aji, & lemon
drop. & lastly c. pubescens

(so named because
of their hairy leaves)

which include rocoto peppers.
Then there are over

thirty
wild species,

just challenging you to collect
(or digest)

every last one
you can.

# Harissa

A chili pepper
paste from North Africa, the word

derives from the Arabic word
*herass*, which refers

to the action of crushing
chilies. Originating

in Tunisia,
a harissa

can be a paste or
a powder,

can be roasted
or dried.

In addition
to the peppers, you'll find

garlic, & spices such as cumin,
paprika, coriander, & salt in

there. & lemon juice.
It's like you

just have to cross a
curry with hot sauce & *voilá*!

# Weaning

It might work for
children, the way that mothers

from the Mexican Kickapoo
tribe smear the juices

of chilies on
their nipples to help wean,

but as for adults… talk about an
invitation on

top of an
invitation!

# Antidote
ßßß
They say *dairy*:
milk, cheese,

sour cream, yogurt,
ice cream, because the fat

dissolves capsaicin. Water
not so much, or beer,

because capsaicin's
an oil, so it doesn't

dissolve in liquid,
but just rides it,

introducing the burn to
new neighborhoods, new

quarters in your mouth, throat,
esophagus. Acid can also

help (tomato, lemon).
Some say pineapple's a fine

chaperone, though really
any relief's

a mirage. The best cure
is time or

another hit
of sauce. Fight

fire with fire, & double
the dosage. A prescription for life: feel

& feel until you're
unable to feel any more.

# Bibliography

Anderson, Heather Arndt. *Chillies: A Global History (Edible)*. Reaktion Books, 2016.

Andrews, Jean. *The Pepper Trail: History and Recipes from Around the World*. University of North Texas Press, 1999.

Andrews, Jean. *The Pepper Lady's Pocket Pepper Primer*. University of Texas Press, 1998.

Campbell, James D. *Mr. Chilehead: Adventures in the Taste of Pain*. ECW Press, 2003.

DeWitt, Dave. *The Chile Pepper Encyclopedia*. William Morrow, 1999.

DeWitt, Dave and Evans, Chuck. *The Hot Sauce Bible*. The Crossing Press, 1996.

DeWitt, Dave and Lamson, Janie. *The Field Guide to Peppers*. Timber Press, 2015.

DeWitt, Dave and Manno, Lois. *Chile Trivia: Weird, Wacky Factoids for Curious Chileheads*. Sunbelt Media, 2012 .

Floyd, David. *101 Chilies to Try Before You Die*. Firefly Books, 2016.

Floyd, David. *The Hot Book of Chillies*. New Holland, 2012.

Garczyynski, Matt. *This is a Book for People Who Love Hot Sauce*. Running Press, 2019.

Kaderabek, Todd. *A Field Guide to Hot Sauces*. Lark Books, 1996.

Nabhan, Gary Paul. *Chasing Chiles: Hot Spots Along the Pepper Trail*. Chelsea Green Publishing, 2011.

Naj, Amal. *Peppers: A Story of Hot Pursuits*. Knopf, 1992.

Nicks, Denver *Hot Sauce Nation, America's Burning Obsession*. Chicago Review Press, 2017.

Robertson, John. *The Hot Sauce Encyclopedia*. 2020.

Schweid, Richard. *Hot Peppers, the Story of Cajuns & Capsaicin*. The University of North Carolina Press, 1987.

Thompson, Jennifer Trainer. *The Great Hot Sauce Book*. Ten Speed Press, 1995.

Walton, Stuart. *The Devil's Dinner, A Gastronomic and Cultural History of Chili Peppers*. St. Martin's Press, 2018.

Stephen Cramer's first book of poems, *Shiva's Drum,* was selected for the National Poetry Series and published by University of Illinois Press. *Bone Music,* his sixth, won the Louise Bogan Award and was published by Trio House Press. He is the editor of *Turn It Up! Music in Poetry from Jazz to Hip-Hop.* His work has appeared in journals such as *The American Poetry Review, African American Review, The Yale Review,* and *Harvard Review.* An Assistant Poetry Editor at *Green Mountains Review,* he teaches writing and literature at the University of Vermont and lives with his wife and daughter in Burlington.